LET'S FIND OUT! COMPUTER SCIENCE

WHAT ARE COMPUTERS?

SARAH MACHAJEWSKI

Britannica Educational Publishing
IN ASSOCIATION WITH
ROSEN
EDUCATIONAL SERVICES

Published in 2018 by Britannica Educational Publishing (a trademark of Encyclopædia Britannica, Inc.) in association with The Rosen Publishing Group, Inc.
29 East 21st Street, New York, NY 10010

Distributed exclusively by Rosen Publishing.
To see additional Britannica Educational Publishing titles, go to rosenpublishing.com.

First Edition

Britannica Educational Publishing
J.E. Luebering: Executive Director, Core Editorial
Mary Rose McCudden: Editor, Britannica Student Encyclopedia

Rosen Publishing
Bernadette Davis: Editor
Nelson Sá: Art Director
Nicole Russo-Duca: Series Designer
Cindy Reiman: Photography Manager
Karen Huang: Photo Researcher

Library of Congress Cataloging-in-Publication Data

Names: Machajewski, Sarah, author.
Title: What are computers? / Sarah Machajewski.
Description: New York : Britannica Educational Publishing, in Association with Rosen Educational Services, 2018. | Series: Let's find out! Computer science | Includes bibliographical references and index. | Audience: Grades 1–4.
Identifiers: LCCN 2017016036| ISBN 9781680488487 (library bound : alk. paper)
| ISBN 9781680488470 (pbk. : alk. paper) | ISBN 9781538300343 (6 pack : alk. paper)
Subjects: LCSH: Computers—Juvenile literature.
Classification: LCC QA76.23 .M33 2017 | DDC 004—dc23
LC record available at https://lccn.loc.gov/2017016036

Manufactured in the United States of America

Photo credits: Cover Anteromite/Shutterstock.com; p. 4 Neirfy/Shutterstock.com; p. 5 Gary Conner/Photolibrary/Getty Images; p. 6 dennizn/Shutterstock.com; p. 7 © 2011 Merriam-Webster, Incorporated; p. 8 © Courtesy of the National Portrait Gallery, London; p. 9 Courtesy of the Moore School of Electrical Engineering, University of Pennsylvania; p. 10 Science & Society Picture Library/Getty Images; p. 11 Apic/Hulton Archive/Getty Images; p. 12 theJIPEN/iStock/Thinkstock; p. 13 iunewind/Shutterstock.com; p. 14 MarkD800/iStock/Thinkstock; p. 15 Teerasak Ladnongkhun/Shutterstock.com; p. 16 Scott Olson/Getty Images; p. 17 Bloomberg/Getty Images; p. 18 Hank Morgan/Science Source/Getty Images; p. 19 © AP Images; p. 20 © Encyclopædia Britannica, Inc.; p. 21 John G. Mabanglo/AFP/Getty Images; p. 22 Cobalt/Fotolia; p. 23 © Courtesy of Apple; p. 24 jannoon028/Shutterstock.com; p. 25 Monty Rakusen/Cultura/Getty Images; p. 26 Akemaster/Shutterstock.com; p. 27 James Steidl/Fotolia; p. 28 Tinxi/Shutterstock.com; p. 29 Aleksandra Suzi/Shutterstock.com; interior pages background © iStockphoto.com/BrianAJackson.

CONTENTS

What Is a Computer?

Playing a game online. Watching a movie on a tablet. Finding a book at the library. On a daily basis, you probably use computers more often than you think! Computers are everywhere, and they're a major part of our lives.

Computers are in our homes, in our classrooms, and in almost any store you can think of. If you have a smartphone, you can even say you have a computer in your pocket. It is hard to imagine a world without computers. But no

All of the devices pictured here are kinds of computers. Some are more mobile than others.

A college math teacher performs a computation on the chalkboard.

one really used what we think of as computers until about 60 years ago. Before that, computers were people who made computations by hand. Today, computers do a lot of tasks, including calculations, for us. Let's find out more about computers.

Think About It

What are some examples of tasks that computers do for us now that we used to do manually?

A computer is a device for working with information. The information can be numbers, words, pictures, movies, or sounds. Computer information is called data. Computers can read huge amounts of data very quickly. They can also store data in files.

Computer technology has been improved to do tasks we want them to perform. For example, early computers could not play videos. Today, the technology that makes that possible is built into all personal computers.

People use computers for fun but also for work. Factory workers use computers to control how things are made. In offices, workers use computers to keep records and to write reports. Computers

Phones can do many things that laptops and desktops can do. So can tablets.

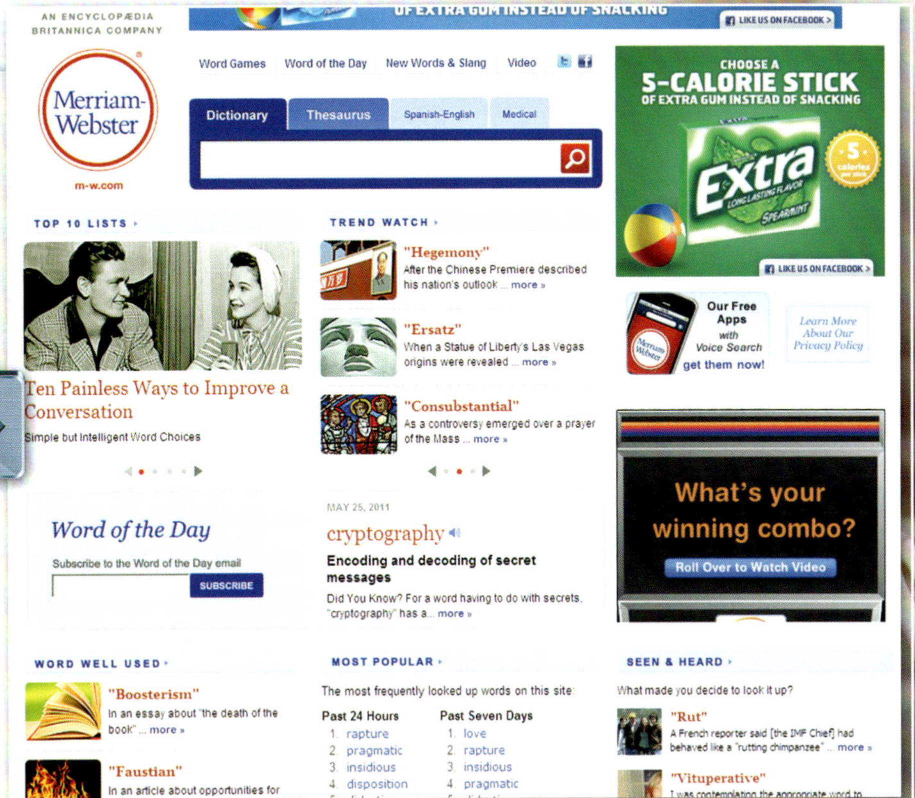

People access websites using the internet. They can learn, shop, and be entertained.

can also help people perform everyday tasks. People use computers for sending email, shopping, and banking. Many people use computers to access the **internet**, which provides information from all over the world.

VOCABULARY

The internet is a communications system that connects computers and computer networks all over the world.

The History of Computers

Computers were invented almost two hundred years ago. An English inventor named Charles Babbage designed the first computer in the 1830s. It was mechanical rather than electronic. Scientists did not yet know how electricity worked. Babbage's idea called for more than 50,000 moving parts. This mechanical device was meant to follow instructions that people entered by using punched cards. However, it was

Charles Babbage designed the Analytical Engine, the forerunner of the modern digital computer.

Compare and Contrast

Sometimes the human brain is called a computer because it also receives and interprets information. How is the brain like a computer? How is it different?

so complex that it was never built during Babbage's lifetime.

In the 1940s, the first electronic computers were introduced. They used electronic switching devices called vacuum tubes. These computers were so big that just one filled an entire room! The cost of these computers was equally large—millions of dollars!

ENIAC was the first all-electronic digital computer.

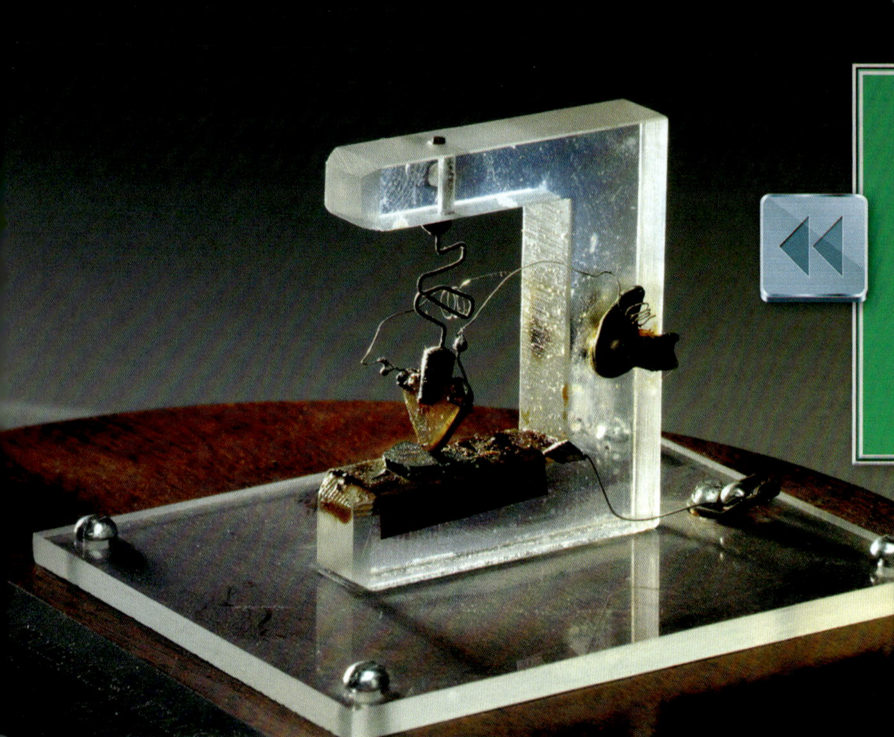

This photo shows the first transistor that ever worked. The first transistors were used in small machines like hearing aids and radios.

Computers improved after a device called a transistor was invented in 1947. A transistor is an electronic switching device. It is used to control the flow of electricity into electronic equipment. The transistor was much smaller and worked better than a vacuum tube. By 1960, transistors had mostly replaced vacuum tubes. Computers became smaller and more affordable than before.

In 1971, American engineer Marcian E. Hoff combined the basic elements of a computer into one tiny chip he called a microprocessor. Early microprocessors

The Intel 4004 was the first microprocessor. It could function as a computer but was produced for a calculator.

THINK ABOUT IT

How did computers becoming smaller and less expensive change the computer industry? Did the smaller size and lower cost help people?

contained thousands of transistors. As microprocessors evolved, more transistors were added, which made computers faster and less expensive.

The introduction of the microprocessor changed the computer industry. Hoff's invention and the hundreds of variations that followed are the computers that operate thousands of modern products. Today, microprocessors are at the heart of almost every electronic computer.

How Computers Work

Most computers are electronic devices, so they work with electricity. Computers get that electricity from a power cord that plugs into a wall or from a battery.

The electricity flows through the computer in electric currents. The thousands or millions of tiny transistors in a microprocessor act as switches. They control how the electric currents flow.

This laptop is powered by a battery located on the underside of the device.

Computers use electric currents to represent the numbers 0 and 1. Computers use strings of those 0s and 1s to stand for letters, sounds, and all of the other data they handle.

VOCABULARY

Electricity is the flow of tiny particles called electrons. It also refers to the energy you get when electrons flow from place to place.

Computers can understand only these patterns of 0s and 1s. All of the instructions that a computer follows have to be in this form. It is hard for people to work with long number patterns, so computer programmers use special languages to write instructions for computers. The computer turns these languages into the number patterns that it can understand.

These patterns of 0s and 1s make up binary code. It is the language of computers.

HARDWARE

A computer's physical parts are called the hardware. All computers have the same basic hardware.

The central processing unit, or CPU, contains a computer's microprocessor. The microprocessor manages all the information that goes into and comes out of the computer. The random-access memory, or RAM, reads programs and data that the microprocessor leaves open.

Most computers only need one microprocessor to function as the CPU.

The internal hard drive (*lower right*) and RAM (*lower middle*) are examples of hardware.

Storage devices hold programs and data. Most computers store information on a hard drive. Hard drives store information on a metal disk inside of the computer.

Input devices allow users to put data and commands into a computer. They include the keyboard and mouse. Output devices allow the user to see or hear a computer's activity. Monitors, printers, and speakers are output devices.

Think About It

Some storage devices, like USB drives, are mobile. This type of device allows users to easily access their data from any computer. Why is this important?

Software

System software can be installed from discs like these. A new computer may already have it installed.

A computer has a brain, and it also uses language in its software. Software is a set of instructions that tell the computer what to do. There are two basic types of computer software: system software and application software.

System software controls how the computer's hardware works together. It does that through an operating system. Its main function is to allow programs to run. Today, most operating systems

The icons you see displayed on this laptop are products of the computer's GUI.

include a graphical user interface, or GUI. The GUI allows a person to communicate with the computer through the use of windows, icons, and menus.

Application software gives the computer instructions for doing a specific task. Playing a game and typing letters are ways of using application software. Smartphone applications, or apps, also allow us to do such fun things as listen to music, play games, shop, and read books.

Compare and Contrast

Describe the similarities and differences between computer hardware and software.

SUPERCOMPUTERS

While some modern computers can fit in your pocket, others can be quite large. Supercomputers are the biggest, most powerful, and fastest computers in existence. The fastest supercomputers can perform many trillions of operations per second. They can do the work of thousands of personal computers. Supercomputers are used for complex work, such as **forecasting** the weather.

Engineering makes these mighty machines possible. Their

VOCABULARY

Forecasting is calculating or predicting a future state or event by examining data.

This is the CM-5 Connection Machine supercomputer. It takes up an amount of space similar to much older computers.

A simulation like this one predicts weather patterns. Scientists share this information with the public.

circuits are kept at temperatures near zero so that their electricity can move almost at the speed of light. And a supercomputer's processors are built and linked to all work on the same problem at once.

As you can imagine, these awesome computers are extremely expensive—some cost billions of dollars. Supercomputers are also extremely large. Some cover the space of two basketball courts!

The PC Revolution

One of the most common types of computers is called a desktop. Desktops are also called personal computers, or PCs. People use desktops in the workplace, at school, and at home. Desktops usually have a monitor, a computer tower or case, a keyboard, a mouse, and a power cord.

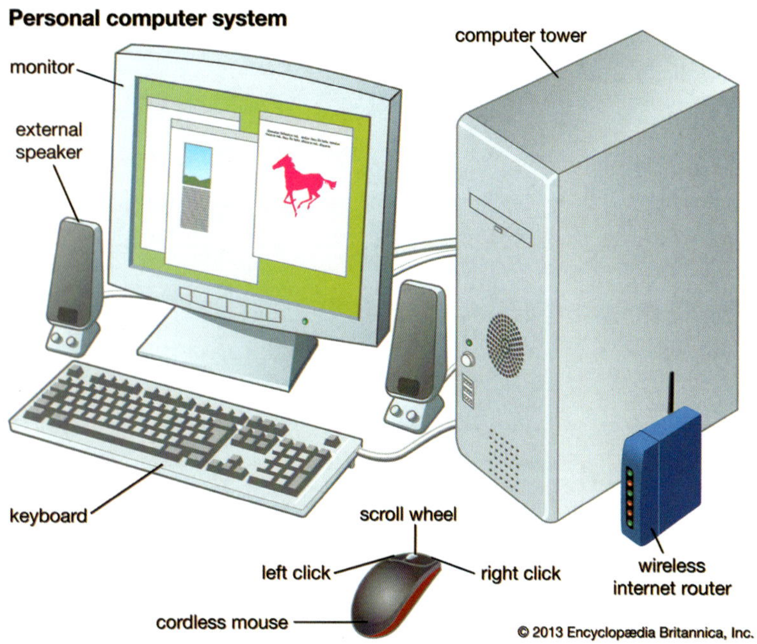

The invention of microchips made personal computers possible. The

This desktop has a monitor, a tower, a keyboard, a mouse, a wireless router, and two speakers.

Think About It

Do you have a computer at home? What do you use it for? What about the computers at school?

first desktop computer for personal use was introduced in 1974. Soon after, Apple Inc. introduced its first desktop computers and IBM introduced the first PC for business use. An era known as the PC Revolution had begun.

The desktop computers we use today are much more powerful and advanced than the business computers of the 1960s and 1970s. Today, PCs can perform billions of operations per second.

Steve Jobs introduces Apple's iMac in 1998. The iMac quickly became the all-time best-selling Mac.

Laptops, Tablets, and Smartphones

A laptop computer contains everything a desktop has, but it's all built into one structure. A laptop screen folds on top of a keyboard and a touchpad (the touchpad works like a mouse). The laptop's hardware and software are beneath the keyboard.

A tablet is a flat touchscreen computer. It's smaller than a laptop and usually bigger than a smartphone. Tablets became popular for personal use after 2010, when Apple introduced a tablet called the iPad. Tablets are used for basic computer tasks, such as using the

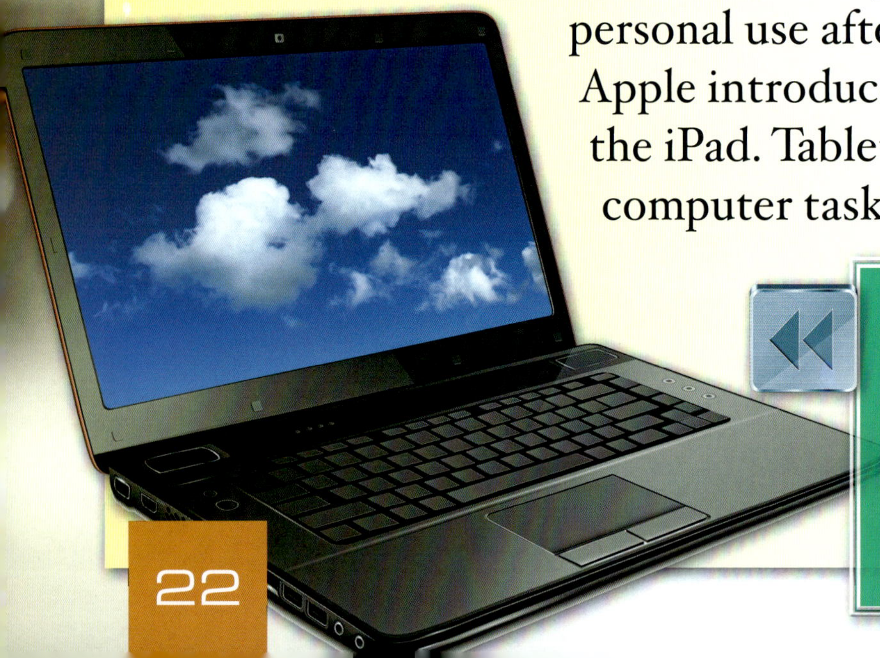

Laptops take up less space than desktops. They can use batteries for power and are portable.

internet, checking email, and watching videos.

Compare and Contrast

Compare and contrast laptops, tablets, and smartphones.

A smartphone is a cell phone that also contains a computer. Smartphones are usually even more mobile than tablets because they tend to be smaller. Users can access the internet, send emails, watch videos, and use countless other apps—all from the same device for making phone calls.

All of these devices run on battery power or can be connected to a power source.

The iPad is a popular Apple product. Apple and other computer companies make tablets in different sizes.

Calculators, Printers, Scanners, and More

Printers connect to a computer to print documents and objects. Some are also able to scan documents.

Did you know the calculator you use for math class is a computer? Calculators have thousands of circuits and thousands or millions of transistors inside them. They tell the calculator how to add, subtract, multiply, and divide. Advanced calculators can do more complicated math.

Printers are commonly used with computers. A user creates

Vocabulary

An **appliance** is a piece of household equipment that performs a particular job and is powered by gas or electricity.

text or an image on a computer and then sends it electronically to a printer. The printer transfers the image or text onto paper. Scanners read images on a printed page and turn them into binary code that a computer can use. The images are then converted to digital files.

Some very small computers control machines. They are built into such things as airplanes, robots in factories, cars, and even household **appliances**. Some of your favorite toys and games may have tiny computers built into them.

In this factory, computers help people run the business. Computers can also control the machines.

What Came Before Computers?

There are some devices that perform calculations but are not computers. These include instruments like an abacus and a slide rule. Even the human brain isn't a computer. However, because of the similarities in the way these things work, people like to compare them to computers.

One machine that performs some of the same functions of a computer is a typewriter. A typewriter is a machine that makes letters on paper when a user hits a key. The key pushes a steel letter against a ribbon covered in ink. The ink from the ribbon then transfers to the paper.

Typewriters were popular from the late 1800s to the late

Calculations on an abacus are made with beads, or counters, that are arranged on wires.

The letters on a computer keyboard are arranged the same way that letters on a typewriter are arranged.

1900s—when personal computers became popular. Computers work much faster and can do more than typewriters. Today, it's rare to see someone use a typewriter. However, the legacy of the typewriter can be seen on the computer keyboard because it uses the same letter arrangement as the typewriter.

Compare and Contrast

Describe how computers and typewriters are similar and different.

An Exciting Future

Whether you're at home playing a game or doing your homework for school, there's a good chance you're using a computer. Computers also keep track of books you borrow from the library and count the cost of purchases at stores and restaurants. There may even be a computer in your refrigerator or your family's car! As you can see, computers come in all shapes and sizes, and they're nearly everywhere.

Video games are run by computer technology. They are popular all over the world.

Virtual reality may be the future of computer technology. Mostly, it is used in video games.

Computer technology has evolved greatly. Everything—from how computers look to how they run—has been tinkered with to become smaller, faster, and capable of doing more than ever before. Computer technology keeps changing every day. There's no telling what the future of computers holds, but it promises to be exciting!

Think About It

If you could invent a computer to do something that helps people, what would it do?

Glossary

advanced Something that is far along in progress or development.

affordable Within someone's ability to pay.

century A period of 100 years.

complex Having many parts, details, ideas, or functions often related in a complicated way.

computation A calculation.

design To think up and draw the plans for; the drawn plan.

device A piece of equipment that serves a special purpose.

era A notable period of history.

evolve To change in a way that creates something distinctly different.

icon A small image on a computer screen that links to a folder, file, or software.

instruction A message that tells a computer to do a certain operation.

manually Done by hand.

mechanical Of or relating to machinery.

smartphone A mobile phone that can install apps and access the internet.

tablet A flat, touchscreen computer.

technology The use of knowledge to invent new devices or tools.

touchscreen A display device that a user operates by touching areas of a screen.

variation A change.

For More Information

Books

Greathead, Helen. *My Smartphone and Other Digital Accessories*. New York, NY: Crabtree Publishing Company, 2017.

Guillain, Charlotte. *Computers. Chicago*, IL: Heinemann Library, 2013.

Hubbard, Ben. *How Computers Work*. North Mankato, MN: Heinemann Raintree, 2017.

Peterson, Megan Cooley. *The First Computers*. North Mankato, MN: Capstone Press, 2015.

Zuchora-Walske, Christine. *What's Inside My Computer?* Minneapolis, MN: Lerner Publications, 2016.

Websites

Because of the changing nature of internet links, Rosen Publishing has developed an online list of websites related to the subject of this book. This site is updated regularly. Please use this link to access this list:

http://www.rosenlinks.com/LFO/Computer

INDEX